Choices, Changes, Chapter and Verse

KATHRYN GRANT

To order additional copies of this book, contact:
Xlibris
844-714-8691
www.Xlibris.com
Orders@Xlibris.com

ISBN: Softcover   979-8-3694-1180-3
         EBook   979-8-3694-1179-7

Library of Congress Control Number: 2023922239

Print information available on the last page

Rev. date: 11/22/2023

Acknowledgements

Below is information to thank all those whose eye for nature's beauty contributed to this effort.

Cover	izzy-gibson-sFrkWv4ACJg-unsplash
Ch. 1	pexels-johannes-plenio-1632790
Ch. 2	flowers-190830_1280
Ch. 3	pexels-pixabay-315987
Ch. 4	flower-827000_1280
Ch. 5	pexels-michael-block-3225518
Ch. 6	pexels-fabio-partenheimer-712398
Ch. 7	owl-1845060_1280
Ch. 8	pexels- gantas-vaičiulėnas-234250
Ch. 9	pexels-tetyana-kovyrina-187928
Ch. 10	Watchman River, sunrise

Introduction

Join a journey that embraces some of life's towering challenges head-on. This book's approach links verbal choices with motivating changes in self and/or environment. Additionally, collaborative chapter and verse selections from scripture and beautiful nature scenes compliment and complete each section. A three-way press to examine personal growth. Every chapter combines these tools, but your specific choices and changes make for a unique and individualized journey. As you interconnect options you designate new and positive pathways, which encourages you to maintain a healthier lifestyle mentally, emotionally, sometimes physically, but above all spiritually.

First, search the contents like a GPS map in order to guide you individually through an unexpected trial or tribulation, because these occur at different times in every person's life. Scroll down and pick your specific area of interest or need on the list. Then embark, navigate, and/or revisit any section as needed down the road. You'll find choices, changes, and dozens of Bible verses for each, as well as delightfully serene photographs to beautifully wrap up each part.

In general all segments mix these ingredients similarly. Verbal exercise choices of encouragement are also humbling and reflective. They are satisfying statements to speak boldly, yet ponder more deeply as you greet each onset anew. Tangible, yet open, activity suggestions contribute to the initial exercises as the catalyst for changes in yourself and your environment. Ultimately though, they are meant to gently persuade emotional and mental systems to catapult forward as well. New parameters start shaping positive goals as realistic, physical outcomes visibly and productively impact growth in all areas of life, when maintained.

Combine these fresh mindsets and empowering opportunities of action 24/7/365 to accelerate knowledge of self and others, but don't stop there. Wisdom, and discernment can deepen, when including scripture, which is gently kneaded into each section as well. Always recite, review, and reprove chapter and verse for reflection and further study. I pray they bring added hope and surprisingly spur you along life's journey. Nevertheless, singular verses are but stepping stones into a full study of God's Word.

Although you may push beyond a current, subjective set of personal mental, emotional, and spiritual perceptions, when completing all three components in conjunction your foundation is reinforced. A combination to build a broader base for healing from application becomes internalized. If you advance in this fashion your personal contribution sheds light on choices and changes that best fit your particular needs and experiences. I pray for any of life's mountains to be movable and all broken pieces become blessings for growth and healing.

Content Sections

Point Me to My Purpose

Choices

- Even if I appear to stand alone with truth, a courageous choice is integral for the firmest foundation. Unlike the shifting sands of falsehood and pretension, this type of strength has a legacy of longevity.

- Even if it appears no one near me cares and/or I don't know how to rise above my current situation, a larger scale purpose beyond myself to benefit others, whether in my community, city, or beyond always exists.

- I choose a more mentally and emotionally balanced center, not by sitting on a fence, but by fixing my focus on goals for the greater good.

- I choose positive people and places to assist, such as teachers, counselors, coaches, or mentors. Attention to their life choices alert me to alternative ideas I've not yet considered or experienced for my own.

- I choose to think and look outside the boxes I have created for myself in the past, because it helps expand options.

- I choose to consider and contemplate all options available, because I can branch out like a giant oak, which extends my sphere of influence and understanding.

- I choose to pursue future expectations in worthwhile projects and purposes, because they add value and character to my life.

- I choose to connect and interact with other positively minded souls, because it is healthier mentally, emotional, physically, and spiritually.

Changes

Change your scope of vision by viewing the resilience, perseverance, and purpose of those in your sphere of interests. Research and be mentored, whether by reading, videos, discussion with others. Someone like Rosa Parks or Daniel from the Bible are example of those who did not back down and change and truth was brought to light. This happens eventually, but your efforts draw attention through an honorable, steadfast position.

Give thought to a bucket list for yourself of people to see and/or meet, music to hear, places to visit and explore, food to taste and/or cook, new skills/talents to study for and/or practice that point to a greater aspiration you have yet to pursue. Now, start a new bucket list to assist others. Open yourself up to those you can help that are in need. A good place to start is your own community, whether family, friends, and/or neighbors. There are always opportunities to volunteer or donate to a homeless shelter, nursing home, animal rescue or church.

Most importantly get grounded in God's creation, so you are emotionally ready for either bucket list. Go for a walk or picnic in a park. Enjoy time by or in the water at the beach, a lake, or a river. If you don't have a pet to nurture, go to a zoo, even a petting zoo, stroll through a pet store, or watch some hilarious animal videos and simply smile at the adorable cuteness and beauty of animals.

Through all of it remember to express what you're thankful and grateful for daily, not just on holidays, whether you celebrate past or present lessons learned or give recognition to blessings. Give thanks in private with friends and family or as a positive post to your social media. Make a list of them and prominently display it on the fridge to remind you, when life gets tough. If friends and family visit and want to share, let them add to the list of gratitude.

Chapters and Verses

Proverbs 23:18-19 For surely there is a future and your hope will not be cut off. 19 Listen, be wise, and guide your mind, heart, and soul on the right path.

Ecclesiates 3:1 To everything there is a season and a purpose under Heaven.

John 16:13 When the Spirit of Truth comes, He will guide you into all the truth, for He will speak on His own authority, but whatever he hears He will speak and He will declare to you all the things that are to come.

1 Corinthians 10:11 But all these things that occurred to them were for our example and it was written for our instruction, on whom the fulfillment of ages has come.

Philippians 3:12 Not that I have already achieved all my goals in this, nor have I already been made perfect in Christ, but press on to take hold of that for which Jesus Christ took hold of me.

1 Peter 4:9-10 Show hospitality to one another without complaining. 10 As good stewards of the manifold Grace of God, each of you should use whatever gift(s) he has received to serve one another.

Fly Beyond Fear and Anxiety

Choices

- Even if I am skeptical of new choices or changes, I am open to trying.

- I choose to look ahead to successes and failures, glory and danger alike; but notwithstanding I move forward.

- I choose positive challenges, which keeps unnecessary fear and anxiety from becoming a domino effect of stress.

- Even if life has constantly shifting cycles of various durations, when I resist or rebel against positive choices and changes, I risk a riptide of drama and extra effort to push forward.

- I choose literal energy increases like a "level-up" for all systems, emotionally, mentally, physically, and above all spiritually.

- Even though my fear is a natural response to unknown or unfamiliar territory, I move forward as a brave soldier. I am not alone, because everyone continues to consistently grow and change, but at different rates.

- Even if I am uncertain or confused about what to say or do, whether in the immediate future and/or years down the road, I can make a decision from an objective, rational analysis of my options.

- Even if my concerns stem from fear of judgement, I now know my actions and reactions are my own not others, when stated and done in love and truth.

- I choose God's Word, partly because it has over 300 verses saying, "do not fear" in one form or another.

- I choose critical thinking skills, because they are the best tool to investigate what I need to say and do with less worry.

- I choose to stop being preoccupied with what others think, because I will then develop an independent, critical, and rational mindset.

Changes

Simplify life in some way in every area of your life. Begin by cleaning out and clearing spaces, literal places in your home and/or work. Rearrange, clean, toss trash from junk drawers, food pantries/ cabinets, all closets, the patio, a balcony, the garage, and/or a backyard shed. Apply to your circumstance... one section at a time. Check back in 6 months to a year to refresh, so it doesn't become overwelming again.

Once all is cleared, consider a relaxing and grounding hobby or side interest that can release stress like cooking, painting, crafting, gardening or adding a feeder to watch take pics of birds. If you want to get more physical, get to work restyling an old car or an old dresser or antique. Be sure to take before an after pics to share with friends and family.

If your ability and stamina level are up to it (or you want to get back in shape), join a class for cross-fit, karate, boxing, cycling, an outdoor survival training course (or make your own in the back yard). You can include the whole family in a simple walk, hike, or bike ride around the block, at the city park, or adventure farther afield to a national park.

Another avenue is to make a list of of outcomes from choices and changes in the past that were stress free. Weigh new choices and changes, even in small measure, to past successful solutions, but continue to add new strategies outside the box. Small moments of success build over a lifetime. Be sure to write down authentic changes in each area you grow and complete. Recording changes safegards any desire to refer back to and/or share your journey of successes with others later.

Chapters and Verses

Psalm 46: 1-3 God is our refuge and strength, an ever-present help in times of trouble. 2 Therefore we will not fear, though the earth is transformed and the mountains are toppled into the depths of the seas,…

Psalm 66:16 Come and listen, all you who fear God, and I will declare what He has done for me. 17 I cried out to Him with my mouth and praised Him with my tongue

Psalm 94:19 When anxiety overwhelms me, Your consolation delights my soul.

Proverbs 12:25 Anxiety in a man's heart weighs him down, but a good word makes him glad.

Proverbs 29:25 The fear of man is a snare, but whoever trusts in the LORD is set securely on high.

Isaiah 41:13 For I am the LORD your God, who takes hold of your right hand and tells you: Do not fear, I will help you.

Matthew 6:34 Therefore do not be anxious about tomorrow, for tomorrow will be anxious for itself. Sufficient for the day is its own trouble.

John 14:27 Peace I leave with you, my peace I give unto you: not as the world giveth, give I unto you. Let not your heart be troubled, neither let it be afraid.

Philippians 4:6 Be anxious about nothing, but in everything, by prayer and supplication with thanksgiving, let your requests be made known to God.

2 Timothy 1:7 For God has not given us a spirit of fear, but of power, love, and self-control.

1 Peter 5:7 Cast all your anxiety on Him, because God cares for you.

Bad Influences Begone

Choices

- Even if there are negative and toxic influences in my life from past choices, attitudes, and behaviors, I can let go of them now. They do not serve my peace, happiness, and/or greater good and future life choices.

- Even if it's painful to let go of certain people, places, and/or things, I accept what I must release to change and create space for someone, some thing, and/or a better environment for peace and growth.

- Even if I am giving and loving, I will not be naive or an emotional, mental, physical, mental, financial, or spiritual doormat. I value my worth and purpose to love and forgive others, but not at the expense of my growth, loyalty, and integrity.

- Even if I want to "fix" someone or a specific situation, I know others must use their own free will to want healthier lifestyle choices.

- Even if there are good memories, I retain them without forgetting the toxic drama and unhealthy choices I must move away from and release to have peace and growth.

- Even if others don't understand or choose to rebel against my new boundaries, I bolster calm confidence and politely say, "No!" Whatever is not positive, uplifting, and respectful of my value and God's greater good is not equally yoked with me and has chosen a different path.

- There I seek out and add to my life, but always after a reasonable time of rational vetting. It is simply common sense to do so.

- Freedom from toxicity and negative drama brings a more peaceful spirit, a mental calm, as well as friendly, encouraging environments.

- I forgive, love, pray, and accept bad influences from a safe distance, so they do not control my choices. I am not in control of the consequenes of their choices.

- I choose to release objects I no longer use, modes of thinking that are outdated, emotional pain from the past, and people who only take and never give.

Changes

Close your eyes and focus on adults, environments, and situations that always take more than they give emotionally, mentally, financially, and above all spiritually. Open your eyes and prepare to step back from as many of those as you can to restore, refresh, and renew in all ways.

Plan measures in all areas and patterns of behavior that do not serve the greater good. Journal your steps as you let go, release, and clear a path to move forward away and apart from anything unhealthy for your mind, body, and soul. This will help you stay on track and remain consistent. Changes may include limiting, modifying, or eliminating something or time with someone altogether. Do them one by one and move forward.

Embrace the challenge to balance energy and include emotionally healthier, happier people and places that exude honesty and integrity in all areas. Some adaptations will be tougher than others, especially if you have to release people to their own path, which diametrically opposes your journey.

Include a list of people, places, and phone numbers to assist and/or go to, when you need a safe and comforting person and/or place. Share this list only with someone you can trust explicitly. Don't hesitate to ask God and His angels to guide, protect, and give you comfort.

Each time you make an important decision, seriously evaluate the choice you're making. Is it really your choice or one you make based off of another's influence? It should not matter so much, if someone likes or agrees with your choice. We are all different. Remember, it's better to be genuine, unique in your attributes, rather than a fake or a copy of another.

Chapters and Verses

Proverbs 13:20 He who walks with the wise will become wise, but the companion of fools will be destroyed.

John 8:12 Once again, Jesus spoke to the people and said, "I am the light of the world. Whoever follows Me will never walk in the darkness, but will have the light of life."

Acts 26:18... Turn from darkness to light and from the power of Satan to God, that you may receive forgiveness of sins and an inheritance among those who are sanctified by faith in me.

1 Corinthians 5:11 But now I am writing you not to associate with anyone who claims to be a brother but is sexually immoral or greedy, an idolater or a verbal abuser, a drunkard or a swindler. With such a man do not even eat.

1 Corinthians 15:33 Do not be deceived: "Bad company corrupts good character."

2 Corinthians 6:17 "Therefore come out from their midst and be separate, says the Lord, and touch nothing unclean, and I will receive you."

2 Galatians 5:19-20 The desires of the flesh are obvious: sexual immorality, impurity, and debauchery; 20 idolatry and sorcery; hatred, discord, jealousy, and rage; rivalries, divisions, factions,...

Ephesians 4:31 Get rid of all bitterness, rage and anger, outcry and slander, along with every form of malice.

2 Timothy 2:22 Flee from youthful passions and pursue righteousness, faith, love, and peace together with those who call on the Lord out of a pure heart. 23 But reject foolish and ignorant speculation, for you know that it breeds quarreling....

Hebrews 13:5 Keep your lives free from the love of money and be content with what you have for God has said, "Never will I leave you, never will I forsake you."

Dissolve the Daze of Deception

Choices

- Even if I did not see the red flags initially, I listen carefully now.

- I choose not to hurt myself by secretly harboring anger or resentment, openly holding on to despair, or purposefully pushing down feelings of bitterness.

- Even if I have been betrayed, I can stand with truth on my lips; and the warmth of integrity and forgiveness to mend my heart.

- If choose to live unashamed of my words, because the integrity of peace, clarity, and truth must guide my life.

- Even if I create a big, messy splash with newly adopted choices, the initial ripple of changes will smooth to calmer waters.

- Even if I accept consequences for my prior bad behavior, I must tell the truth.

- Even if I have not been honest with myself or others, I know it's never too late to come clean and right a wrong with both words and actions. This is the only way to heal deep deception within myself or others.

- Even if telling the truth is embarrassing, that is temporary. The truth is always eternal and keeps you at peace with decisions.

- I choose to practice being a good communicator, so I am in control of what and how I speak

-Even if I think I might hurt someone's feelings or they might be upset with me, warranted or not, state your truth kindly and with love.

- I choose to mean what I say and say what I mean, because sarcasm is a lie with a hint of ugly truth. Be kind.

-I choose to live healthy without confusion or guilt that sits stuffed inside my head and heart.

- I choose to be honest and refuse to continue to cover up lies I've already told.

- I choose to grow and mature emotionally, because love does not manipulate other people and/or situations for self serving needs and desires.

- I choose to serve the greater good in love for all involved, including self, but never just self or to put self above others.

- I choose truth, because lies create a cracked and fragmented reflection. I no longer choose to hide behind a mask, so I can see my authentic self in the mirror.

Changes

Set firm boundaries and keep them to free yourself to grow and mature mentally, emotionally, and above all spiritually. Not only speak truth in all ways, but expect it in return. Once a lie comes into being, whether of omission, a twist of truth, and/or an out right falsehood. Do not enable lies.

Words carry weight and meaning and add value to self. Words devalue self as well as others, if deceit spews forth. Deception like gossip is easy to speak, but causes damage like throwing a stone and hiding your hands. Lies show immaturity and stop growth in all areas of self. Not one relationship remains whole and growing, when deceit or betrayal prospers.

Apologies and truth begin to rectify deception. Extending a simple, lame, "I'm sorry." without the truth of what the perpetrator is sorry for or why keeps a lie alive. Time is wasted for a liar and others involved. Being honest with yourself grows confidence to change and help heal those that are hurt. (All lies hurt.) Start with self before addressing another's issues. Here is a simple exercise to reflect and lay bare intentions.

Fold a paper lengthwise in half. On one side list lies you've told. Start with the most current, on-going, and/or obvious lies. Ego must be set aside as you work backward into your past from the present; and keep moving on down the page. On the side across from the false statements and actions, write what you should have said or done, as well as how to rectify and heal the issue to bring balance as closely as possible. Do it personally, not through others and without blame toward others. Ask God to guide you with words of wisdom.

No one is flawless or perfect in any area, so it's okay to recognize problems, mistakes, and lies. Initially, it may hurt to see, but being authentic puts you in good company. Muster courage to step forth in your new healthier lifestyle choices and changes, even if some past companions scatter. Lessons learned must be practiced to internalize and some may not understand.

Do not enable vague, generalized responses or excuses. Liars mask and manipulate self, not just others, by trying to make self look better. Behavior patterns develop quickly, but take work to cultivate. Put that same time, effort, and intelligence into speaking with integrity and honesty. Mend the broken fence of any lie that slips out to heal yourself and mature.

Chapters and Verses

Exodus 20: 16 You shall not bear false witness...

Proverbs 12:22 Lying lips are an abomination to the Lord, but those who act faithfully are a delight.

Jeremiah 17:9 The heart is more deceitful than anything else. It is sick. Who can clearly understand it.

Acts 5:4... why hast thou conceived this thing in thine heart? thou hast not lied unto men, but unto God.

Ephesians 4:29 Let no unwholesome talk come out of your mouths, but only what is helpful for building up the one in need and bringing grace to those who listen.

Colossians 3:9-10 Do not lie to one another, since you have taken off the old self, practices and habits 10 Put on the new self, which is renewed in knowledge in the image of the Creator.

Colossians 4:6 Leet your speech always be gracious, seasoned with salt, so that you may know how to answer everyone.

James 1:22 Be doers of the word, not hearers only, otherwise you are deceiving yourself.

1 Peter 3:11 If anyone speaks, he should speak as one conveying the words of God. If anyone serves, he should serve with the strength God provides, so that in all things God may be glorified through Jesus Christ, to whom be the glory and the power forever and ever.

Build Bridges, Buttress Burdens

Choices

- Even if burdens of life are large, I place them in order of priority and complete each part brick by brick, so my foundation becomes stronger.

- Even if I burned one or more bridges in the past, I will walk in faith through dark circumstances to the light of truth and rebuild with lessons learned.

- Even if I lost my job or I am in a financial crisis, I have skills, talents, and perseverence to apply toward new and prosperous goals.

- Even if I've made mistakes, missed a deadline, and/or made a mess of a situation, I take accountibility and responsibility now to repair, redo, and heal all areas of my life.

- Even I have not managed my money and other responsibilities like I should, I know what I want is not always what I need.

- I choose to work hard and continue to have faith and serve, because I know God will provide what I need, not what I want, in His time.

- I choose to realistically view and practically approach all situations, places, and people, so I can clear my conscience without blaming others.

- I choose to consider ALL my options, even ones I don't want long term, but are stepping stones to brighter, future goals.

- I choose to work smarter, not harder. I choose to revamp, retrain, and/ or rebuild to plan anew in the present.

- I choose to keep trying and get up, if I fall down or miss my initial mark.

- I choose to spend within my means, pay off my debts, and set a weekly budget and stick to it.

Changes

To build a bridge you need a blueprint. If you had one and the bridge burned, blew up, or crumbled under it's own weight, you need to change your prior plans and reassess where things went wrong...without blaming others first... or possibly at all. Should you choose to repair or build a new bridge over rough waters, begin a list of resources to design that new draft for your success.

Realize first and foremost mistakes, even failures, reveal lessons for all involved. Learn yours, so you don't repeat it! If you attribute blame to others, you are not reflecting to evaluate self. You will not grow emotionally and will eventually find yourself in the same cycle; ultimately being tested again to finally mature. Growth in any area builds a firmer foundation for a future to be celebrated.

Humility graciously admits and accepts their part from beginning to end in the lessons not yet learned. Pride and ego are put on the back burner to receive knowledge and wisdom. If you still need to do this, forgive yourself to the consequences already in play and commit seriously to changes in all areas, mentally, emotionally, financially, and above all spiritually. Now you are ready to move forward with this enlightened perspective about yourself and toward all new ventures.

Write down or make a vision board of all your realistic skills, talents and available, viable options. (Spy or superhero should not be on your list.) Choose one for a focus, even if you have to do another job, while you study and practice for a different field or career. You may even cultivate or expand an existing hobby or artistic pursuit.

Cut back and cut out unnecessary gadgets, toys, and entertainment. The goal is long term success, not immediate, impulsive rewards. Keep receipts for accountability to self and others effected. Keep them in a book or file. Most importantly share your plans and goals with family and friends who encourage your new choices. This can remind them and you that your behavior has changed for the better... long term. Lastly, offer a service or repayment schedule to clear debts to family, friends, and/or companies. Stick to it and your bridges will be repaired or rebuilt strong and beautiful.

Chapters and Verses

Psalm 37:23-25 The steps of a man are ordered by the LORD who takes delight in his journey. 24 Though he falls, he will not be hurled headlong for the LORD is holding his hand. 25 I once was young and now am old, yet never have I seen the righteous abandoned or their children begging for bread.

Psalm 55:22 Throw down all your burdens before the Lord and He will sustain you.

Psalm 62:10 Place no trust in extortion, or false hope in stolen goods. If your riches increase, do not set your heart upon them.

Proverbs 24:16 Though a righteous man may stumble and fall seven times, he still gets up; but the wicked stumble in bad times.

Jeremiah 29:11 I know the plans I have for you declares the Lord; plans to prosper you and not to harm you and to give you a future and a hope.

Matthew 5:41 Whoever compels you to go one mile with them, go with them two miles.

Matthew 11:28-29 Come to Me, all you who are weary and burdened, and I will give you rest. 29 Take My yoke upon you and learn from Me; for I am gentle and humble in heart, and you will find rest for your souls.

Luke 6:3Give and it will be given to you. A good measure, pressed down, shaken together and running over. It will be poured into the bosom of your lap.

1 Corinthians 3:14-15 If what he has built survives, he will receive the reward. 15 If it is burned up, he will suffer loss. He will be saved, but only as if through flames (to refine).

1 Corinthians 9:24 Do you not know that in a race all the runners run; but only one receives the prize? Run in such a way as to take the prize.

Philippians 4:19 Moreover my God shall supply all your needs according to His riches and Glory by Jesus Christ.

1 Timothy 6:17 Instruct those who are rich in the present age not to be conceited and not to put their hope in the uncertainty of wealth, but in God, who richly provides all things for us to enjoy.

Let Go My Ego

Choices

- I choose to learn from my mistakes and own my mishaps.

- Even though mistakes and mishaps happen, I allow myself to gain new perspectives, so I can grow in all areas of life.

- I choose to recognize the reality of imperfections, not only in myself, but in everyone, but God.

- Even if I am not in control of a situation currently, I choose to accept that I can step back and evaluate, reassess, renew composure.

- I choose to let God guide my choices, thoughts, and actions, instead of the world or others in my sphere of influence.

- Even if I lost control of my emotions outwardly in anger or by stuffing my emotions in silence in the past, I can choose to breathe and communicate calmly, rationally, and realistically.

- Even if I think or feel I need to "fix" someone and/or a situation, I know people must use their own free will to grow in any area of their life.

- I choose to forgive, love, pray, and accept others who refuse to change and grow or mature mentally, emotionally, financially, and above all spiritually from a safe distance.

- I choose to recognize I am not in control of the consequences and choices of other adults, nor are they in control of me or mine as an adult.

- I choose to see from a perspective of humility over my desires, so I can learn, grow, and mature in all areas of self.

- I choose to recognize and heal emotional and spiritual pain, so those areas of my life grow at the same rate as my mental intelligence.

- I choose to be responsible for my own emotions, behaviors, and actions in all areas of life as an adult, instead of blaming others.

- I choose to move forward in realistic love that does not compete or hold onto grudges and bitterness.

- I choose to change negative and/or pessimistic patterns of behavior, so I have hope, positivity, and peace for the future.

- I choose to let go of victimized feelings, reckless thoughts, and/or fleeting pleasures, whether physical or financial, so a more lasting peace and order can occur and be mantained.

Changes

Life has constantly shifting cycles, some short and some long. Resisting change can lead you into a a new cycle like a harsh riptide can pull you under or push against forward movement. Opposing your own personal growth stunts maturity in one or multiple areas and creates unecessary stressors. Doctors, counselors, therapists, and psychologists have written volumes of studies in the last 100 years attesting to the fact that, if lack of growth continues in any area, physical illness manifests and fester in the body, as well as the possibility for environamental disorder ensuing and mounting in the home environment.

I can hear Michael Jackson singing from Man in the Mirror. "If you wanna make the world a better place, take a look at yourself and then make that change." A place to start is to make sure you mean what you say and say what you mean. Listen to what you say and how you say it. Record yourself as needed. Sarcasm usually masks a negative response to truth you have chosen to state in a passive aggressive way. Speak with sincere kindness and integrity. Refer back to your "choice" statements for some guidance.

Now that you have listened to self, consider actions that back up your statements. Do you follow through with what you say? Intentionality is key. Do you intend to do what you say? Are you just trying to please others or keep a false peace? Ill will only serves self and is a solution that belies reality for your benefit only in the end. A bad behavior pattern that leads to broken promises and ultimate exposure of betrayal unhappy relationships. Practice statements that are not vague or generalized. Be specific and honest. If you don't intend to do something, don't say that you will.

Be the example to yourself, then to others by association. There is no validation for feeling ashamed, when words and actions do not match. Write post-it notes of positive behavior words and actions like "Listen to others views and think, instead of speaking first." Add more or include some of your favorite choice statements. Commit further to these changes by placing them prominently in areas you see daily like your fridge, laptop, bathroom mirror, microwave, car dashboard, etc. Set these new parameters and boundaries of behavior to prepare for distractions and temptations. Those things cloud and hinder growth. Ask God for guidance each time.

Chapters and Verses

Proverbs 3:5-6 Trust in the Lord with all your heart and lean not on your own understanding 6 In all your ways acknowledge Him and He will make your path straight.

Proverbs 11:11-13 By the blessing of the upright a city is built up, but by the mouth of the wicked it is torn down. 12 Whoever despises his neighbor lacks wisdom, but a man of understanding remains silent. 13 A gossip reveals a secret, but a trustworthy person keeps a confidence.

Proverbs 18:12 Before his downfall a man's heart is proud, but humility comes before honor.

Ecclesiastes 7:8-9 The end of a matter is better than the beginning and a patient spirit is better than a proud one. 9 Do not be quickly provoked in your spirit for anger resides in the heart of fools.

Mark 11:25 And when you stand to pray, if you hold anything against another, forgive it, so that your Father in Heaven will forgive your tresspasses as well.

Romans 13:12 The night is nearly over and the day has drawn near, so let us lay aside the deeds of darkness and put on the armor of light.

2 Corinthians 10:13-14 We, however, will not boast beyond our limits, but only within the field of influence that God has assigned to us a field that reaches even to you. 14 We are not overstepping our bounds, as if we had not come to you. Indeed, we were the first to reach you with the gospel of Christ

Ephesians 6:12 For our struggle is not against flesh and blood, but against principalities, rulers, the darkness of this world, and spiritual hosts of wickedness in heavenly places.

James 3:2 We all make mistakes. For if we could control our tongues, we would be perfect and could also control ourselves in every other way.

James 4: 1-2 what causes conflicts and quarrels among you? Don't they come from the passions at war within you? 2 You crave what you do not have. You quarrel and fight. You do not have, because you do not ask. 3 And when you do ask, you do not receive, because you ask with wrong motives, that you may squander it on your pleasures.

Triumph Against Trauma and Abuse

Choices

- Even if I have been hurt emotionally, verbally, and/or physically, I choose to value all of who I am and what I do on earth mentally, emotionally, financially, and above all spiritually, especially in God's eyes.

- Even if an environment, whether home, business, or community, or people in those environments created fear or trauma, I can release it in the present and future; because it does not serve my greater good.

- Even if I experienced trauma and/or abuse in the past, whether as a very young child, a teen, or an adult, in the present I choose to heal by forgiving and loving myself and others, so I can grow and mature mentally, emotionally, physically, and above all spiritually.

- I choose to move forward by showing and sharing love, kindness, caring, and happiness, as I forgive persecution from my past and present.

- I choose to persevere to a place of safety and peace.

- I choose to never settle to be less than loved with reciprocal kindness, nurturing, and support in all my relationships, whether friends, family, and/or business.

- I choose encouraging words and activities that inspire positive change and happiness in all areas of my life

- I no longer choose situations and relationships that are chaotic, harsh, irrational, or lacking in integrity.

- In all areas of life I choose to heal, so I am balanced emotionally,. mentally, and above all spiritually.

- Even if I choose love and light, I must move to protect myself and keep myself and others safe.

-Even if there are financial losses, begin to make plans to stop and leave toxic relationships and all interactions, if possible. Safety and peace are more important than worldly possessions.

Changes

-Consider meeting with professionals like a counselor, pastor, safe house, lawyer, and/or detective to discuss your concerns, as fits your need.

- Write a letter of love and encouragement to the wounded warrior or inner child within your mind and heart.

- Write a letter of encouragement to your future adult self in the present and looking toward future goals for healing and maturity. Work toward them.

- Assist healing in self by helping others like you. Make a personal change in an area(s) of interest to you. Here are a some to consider. Give some food, clothes, and or time to a women's shelter. Volunteer time at a homeless shelter, animal rescue, or an old folks home as a singer, comedian, or book reader.

Recognize "red flags" by listening and obseving behaviors carefully. Then, unashamedly set boundaries for yourself and stick to them. Write them down and post them around your house, if you need to be reminded. This can help you love and forgive others without returning to those who mean harm mentally, emotionally, and/or physically through deceit like a wolf in sheep's clothing. Also listen, when others give vague and/ or generalized statements, excuses, and/or responses to questions. Hold others accountable and responsible for their words and behaviors. Continue to study behavior patterns of others who may attempt to pull you back and continue the abuse down the road. Stand firm in all boundaries you've set. Don't give in to tears.

Rid yourself of all toxic people, places, behaviors, and lifestyle choices, so that you can stand confident in your mindset choices and changes. Simply saying, "No." calmly and confidently may need to become a more common word in your vocabulary. Sometimes it is about reprogramming your mind, emotions, and verbal reactions to dissolve or at least dissapate prior patterns of people pleasing, enabling bad behaviors from others or being a doormat.

Survivors thrive through living and persevering, not giving in or giving up.

When others are abusive and bullying leave the area without any announcement, explanation, and/ or apology. Walk, run, and/or call 911, if you ever feel unsafe. Record and remain calm. Ask help from neighbors, family, and/or friends, but above all ask God for His guidance and protection. The Holy Spirit is the salt which can season personal safety 24/7/365.

Chapters and Verses

Deuteronomy 31:6 So be strong and courageous! Do not be afraid and do not panic before them. For the LORD your God will personally go ahead of you. He will neither fail you nor abandon you.

Psalm 10:17-18 O Lord, you hear the desire of the afflicted; you will strengthen their heart; you will incline your ear to do justice to the fatherless and the oppressed, so that man who is of the earth may strike terror no more.

Psalm 11:5 The LORD tests the righteous and the wicked; His soul hates the lover of violence.

Psalm 30: 5... Weeping may last through the night, but joy comes with the morning.

Psalm 60:11-12 Give us aid against the enemy, for the help of man is worthless. 12 With God we will perform with valor, and He will trample down our enemies.

Proverbs 16:32 He who is slow to anger is better than a warrior, and he who controls his temper is greater than one who captures a city.

Proverbs 17:14-15 To start a quarrel is to release a flood, so abandon the dispute before it greaks out. 15 Acquitting the guilty and condemning the righteous – both are destestable to the Lord.

Isaiah 41:11 Behold, all who rage against you will be ashamed and disgraced; those who contend with you will be reduced to nothing and will perish.

Mark 9:42 But if anyone causes one of these little ones who believe in Me to stumble, it would be better for him to have a large millstone hung around his neck and to be thrown into the sea.

John 10:10 The thief comes only that he might steal and might kill and might destroy. I came that they may have life, and may have it abundantly.

2 Corinthians 10:4 The weapons of our warfare are not the weapons of the world. Instead, they have divine power to demolish strongholds.

Colossians 3:19 Husbands and wives love one another and do not treat each other harshly.

Ephesians 5:8 For at one time you were in darkness, but now you are in the light of the Lord. Walk as children of light.

Garner Grace through Illness and Grief

Choices

- Even if internal and/or external challenges exist from the past or remain in the present, I know I can express and calmly release healthy thoughts and emotions, whether saddness or anger and return to peace.

- Even though I feel confusing thoughts or grief, I slowly take a deep breath in and out, look up and around outside a window or in nature (day or night) and realize there is a world more beautiful and bigger than me to recognize and absorb.

- I choose to breath in positive and happy experiences each day, along with other emotions, so I can grow and mature.

- Even though I may have tremendous pain now, I ask for help to ease and/or alleviate the stress, burdens, and/or physical hurt presently and for the future.

- Even if assistance is given in ways I don't always realize, in ways I may not see, understand, or expect, I am open to various possibilities and choices in all areas.

- Even if the diagnosis is not positive, but I am still breathing in this present moment, then I accept I have purpose on this earth and lessons to learn about myself and/or others on this journey with me.

- A new or additional purpose in life can be expressed, if I simply ask God to give more wisdom and discernment, so it is revealed to me in faith, hope, and love.

- Even if I cannot speak, God hears my prayers.

- If I am still alive, I have purpose for myself, my friends, my family, and my community, because there are lessons to learn for me and/or them.

- I choose to rise above illness and grief by listening and/or watching upbeat music, movies, and/or books. Laughter truly is the best medicine.

- Even if it is just a walk around the block or opening the blinds each day, suck up a bit of sunshine. It is healthy in more ways than one.

Changes

Write a list or share a list verbally about things you are passionate about changing for the better, in family, community, or even on a larger scale. Choose one of those objectives to focus on helping. Begin a plan to initiate your steps to improve whatever area want to make that change. Recognize a life purpose does not have to include grand gestures, although those ripple effects are not often seen right away. Sometimes the smallest gesture is paid forward reaching an unknown, farther shore...even years away.

Here are a few ideas to get started. Open a foundation, charity or shelter/ rescue in someone's name. Plant a tree at a park in remembrance of a life well lived. Consider a book, video, or podcast, where you and others in your situation to share testimony of recovery that helps others.

Now add what you can do by yourself and who and what you need assistance to engage your proposal or project. This new list may include family, neighbors, friends, church or outreach community members, and even on-line support agencies with names and phone numbers. Also include in your solution should prioritize issues and needs, as well as short and long term solutions. Consider all areas of emotional, mental, physical, financial, and above all spiritual issues and obligations. Consult professionals and consider all options and solutions, even those outside the norm in your initial approach.

Keep a notebook, journal, or diary. If you can't write, verbally record it or ask someone to write as you dictate. If you are more artistic, consider a collage, painting, or diorama to represent overcoming your challenges. Along the way, you may have to change an option, adapt it by inreasing/ decreasing and/or look for another purpose outside the box; just do it. A flower goes through constant change, ever opening and beautiful in each moment. You can adapt, if need be. God is in control.

Chapters and Verses

Psalm 34:17-19 The righteous cry out, and the LORD hears. He delivers them from all their troubles. 18 The LORD is near to the brokenhearted; He saves the contrite in spirit. 19 Many are the afflictions of the righteous, but the LORD delivers him from them all.

Lamentations 3:21-23 Yet I call this to mind, and therefore I have hope: 22 Because of the loving devotion of the LORD we are not consumed, for His mercies never fail. 23 They are new every morning; great is Your faithfulness.

Matthew 5:4 Blessed are those who mourn, for they will be comforted.

John 14:1-3 Don't let your hearts be troubled. Trust in God, and trust also in me. 2 There is more than enough room in my Father's home. If this were not so, would I have told you that I am going to prepare a place for you? 3 And if I go to prepare a place for you, I will come and get you, so that you will always be with me where I am.

Romans 8:33-35 Who will bring any charge against God's elect? It is God who justifies. 34 Who is there to condemn us? For Christ Jesus, who died, and more than that was raised to life, is at the right hand of God— and He is interceding for us. 35 Who shall separate us from the love of Christ? Shall trouble or distress or persecution or famine or nakedness or danger or sword?

1 Corinthians 15:49-51 And just as we have borne the likeness of the earthly man, so also shall we bear the likeness of the heavenly man. 50 Now I declare to you, brothers, that flesh and blood cannot inherit the kingdom of God, nor does the perishable inherit the imperishable. 51 Listen, I tell you a mystery: We will not all sleep, but we will all be changed— 52 In an instant, in the twinkling of an eye, at the last trumpet. For the trumpet will sound, the dead will be raised imperishable, and we will be changed.

2 Corinthians 1:4-6 (God) who comforts us in all our troubles, so that we can comfort those in any trouble with the comfort we ourselves have received from God. 5 For just as the sufferings of Christ overflow to us, so also through Christ our comfort overflows. 6 If we are afflicted, it is for your comfort and salvation; if we are comforted, it is for your comfort, which accomplishes in you patient endurance of the same sufferings we experience.

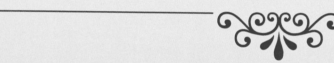

Dare to Lighten Depression's Load

Choices

- Even if balancing life hits like a slap in the face sometimes, it is not to defeat, but to teach and restore correction.

- I choose to ask tough questions, because a sincere pursuit of the truth frees our mind and heart from uncertainty.

- Even if there are trials, in due course change is inevitable, so I look forward with a heart of courage toward all new beginnings.

- I choose positive thoughts, spaces, people and places, because where the mind goes the body follows.

- I choose to forgive and pray for those that don't have my best interest at heart, even if at a distance.

- I choose a well intentioned purpose that has meaning to me, but is for others outside and/or beyond myself.

- I choose to make my house, car, work space, garage, shed, etc. as clean, clear, and simplified as I want my mind and heart to be.

- Even if there are tragic issues bringing my thoughts to negative places, all life has a purpose to better others and I will focus on that.

- I choose to make lemons out of lemonade by adding sweetness and clean water of life's positive opportunities and options.

- I choose more wisely by breathing through each test.

- Even if I to accept laborious responsibilities and/or accountibility for any consequences, God works all for the greater good. Blessings are found in the benefit and brings peace along it's path.

- I choose to get out of my own way and give all problems to God, yet always stop to smell the flowers to remind me of the beauty in God's creation.

Changes

Place your hand on your heart or check your pulse on your wrist or neck, if your heart is still beating and you are still breathing, you still have a purpose. It means God is not finished with you yet. Whether you fullfill your purpose on your own or with others, do it. Your purpose always has to do with whatever skills, trade, degree, and/or life experiences you already have or are capable of doing. Make a realistic list of them, even the minor ones.

Now to begin with the freshest of starts, some prep work in your environment has to be done. Look around and think about how to change it to bring sweetness and the clean water of positivity to your spaces. Add that sweetness through cleaning, clearing, and simplifying where you live and work. Also add sweetness through a softer approach of breathing calmly and keeping your choices clear like clean water, not flakey.

Make three boxes, bags, or areas to separate decisions about all things, a keep pile, a donate pile, and a toss it to the trash pile or the past. Start with your physical environment. Go through clothes first, then objects you haven't touched in 6 months and proceed to each room, closet, pantry, and drawer as you apply this method. Once you've done the inside areas, move to the outside spaces. Every area cleared and cleaned will give you more freedom and positivity, If the amount of work is overwelming, do a little at a time, ask for help, and/or hire a cleaning service to assist.

Changes are a free will choice. How badly do you want to heal and remove chaos and dysfunction from your life. Cue up your favorite positive music as you clean and clear. Once done, quiet all noise and distractions for at least 15 minutes daily. Sit in the stillness of peace and tranquility and the areas for new positive evergy to flow in the spaces created. Express gratitude and give thanks aloud to all who participated. If you did it on your own, take time to nurture yourself with calm panpering, as budget allows, even if it is a hot bath with a cool glass of water, maybe even a couple of candles.

Now go back to your list of items to expand on and/or develop into a purpose outside yourself. If your resources are limited, start by helping others in their purpose that is similar to yours. Look online or in your community or neighborhood first. There are always shelters for people and animal rescue facilities that need help. Allow your interests to grow.

Chapters and Verses

Psalm 23:4 Even though I walk through the darkest valley, I will fear no evil for you are with me. Your rod and your staff comfort me.

Proverbs 3:6 In all your ways acknowledge Him and He will make your paths straight.

Proverbs 15:13-15 A joyful heart makes a cheerful countenance, but sorrow of the heart crushes the spirit. 14 A discerning heart seeks knowledge, but the mouth of a fool feeds on folly. 15 All the days of the oppressed are bad, but a cheerful heart has a continual feast.

Isaiah 40: 29-31 He gives power to the faint and increases the strength of the weak. 30 Even youths grow tired and weary; and young men stumble and fall. 31 But those who wait upon the LORD will renew their strength; they will mount up with wings like eagles; they will run and not grow weary, they will walk and not faint.

Jeremiah 29:11 For I know the thoughts that I think toward you, says the LORD, thoughts of peace and not of evil, to give you a future and a hope.

Romans 5:3-5 Not only that, but we also rejoice in our sufferings, because we know that suffering produces perseverance. 4 Perseverance produces character and hope. 5 And hope does not disappoint us, because God has poured out His love into our hearts through the Holy Spirit, whom He has given us.

1 Corinthians 10:13... God is faithful; He will not let you be tempted beyond what you can bear. But when you are tempted, He will also provide an escape, so that you can stand up under it.

Philippians 3:13-15... Forgetting what is behind and straining toward what is ahead, 14 I press on toward the goal to win the prize of God's heavenly calling in Christ Jesus. 15 All of us who are mature should embrace this point of view. And if you think differently about some issue, God will reveal this to you as well.

Philippians 4:11-13 I am not saying this out of need, for I have learned to be content regardless of my circumstances. 12 I know how to live humbly, and I know how to abound. I am accustomed to any and every situation— to being filled and being hungry, to having plenty and having need. 13 I can do all things through Christ who gives me strength.

Cultivate Character to Nurture Self

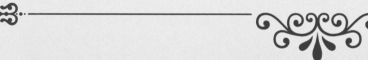

Choices

- I choose a perpetual attitude of gratitude.
- Even if I want the love and acceptance of others, I have to nurture and heal myself to become confident without arrogance.
- I choose to associate with those who put God first and have my best interest at heart.
- I choose to release adults and situations that are toxic, fake, and/or unhealthy for my emotional and mental health.
- I choose relationships that show and share love with reciprocal giving and receiving.
- I choose boundaries that are healthy and stick to them in all ways.
- Even if "self" reliance rings like a bell to the world, it cracks wide open as ego centered; so I choose God reliance, which seeks Him first with humilty and service for the highest and greater good.
- I choose to have a purpose for others beyond myself.
- Even if I am different than most, diversity adds a uniqueness and interest inside and out.
- Even if someone speaks unkindly to me, I do not have to respond in the same manner. Broken, hurt, and insecure people do not define me.
- I choose to be the best example of myself for my family, my friends, those in my community, as well as any strangers I meet along the way.
- Even if I've had a bad day, I can still muster encouragement for myself and others, because that is how God's light is expanded and shared in all areas, emotionally, mentally, physically, financially, and above all spiritually.
- I choose to accept how I look, even if others do not accept me as I am.
- I choose a happy, healthy, and authentic perspective of my body and my style.
- Even if I have scars or other body differences in shape, size, and/or color, that have happened along my journey, all of who I am represents God's purpose in me.
- I choose to recognize the beauty in all people, animals, and places in God's creation, so I shall not focus so much on the flaws.
- I choose to recognize we are all broken, but wonderfully and fearly made.

Changes

If someone says, "Take the high road!" what does it mean? Words like honor, ethics, morals, integrity, love, maybe even minding your own business may come to mind. In all things consider what is the higher road in this situation? Do not think this entails being a doormat. In fact you are doing the exact opposite, when you cultivate character. You do not lay down and give in or give up, you stand in the truth, tall and firmly grounded.

How can you get more grounded? Literally get up, get outside as much as possible, breath in the air, look at God's creation, and realize creation is bigger than us. Take a walk down the street or around the block. If you can go farther, bike, hike or jog in your community, in nature, through a park or on a beach. Pay attention to trees, plants, wildlife, even the stars at night. Consider 10-20 minutes a day to get grounded, oxygenated, and rejuvenated. Go alone, with a partner, with a pet, or join a ramblers group. If you are fit, join a hiking or runners meet-up group... or start one of your own.

Develop nature photography, gardening, cooking or other healthy skill. If you can begin a small personal and/or community garden that's worderful, but getting grounded is simply about taking time to smell the roses and watch the sunset... or sunrise. It's about stepping back from noise, distractions, and/or electronics to destress, decompress, and refresh. Move to calm waters.

Another approach shifts stagnancy to do the same as getting outside, but inside your living area. Move a few items of furniture or décor around, which costs no money. If you can, make or invest in new pillows, pillow covers, throws or light a scented candle. Add some plants or flowers to a windowsill. Display your updated photo gallery. If you need to clean and clear a space and send some items to the Goodwill or simply trash old, unused items, do it.

Once you're more grounded, you can expand your character growth further. Shift priorities to cultivate more love and wisdom through a purpose outside of yourself. What has meaning for you, but gives service to others? Maybe it will be that community garden, a Bible study group, or a making a bunch of pillows to take to the homeless shelter. Try to generate experiences that include people and healthy lifestyle choices to enrich character for all involved. God's guidance can lead the way and assist. Remember, it doesn't have to be a grand gesture; just get started and maintain momentum.

Chapters and Verses

1 Samuel 16:7... Humans do not see what the Lord sees. Humans see what is visible, but the Lord sees the heart.

Job 34:19 Who is not partial to princes and does not favor rich over poor? For they are all the work of His hands.

Proverbs 4:19-21 The way of the wicked is like the darkest gloom; they do not know what makes them stumble. 20 My son, pay attention to my words; incline your ear to my sayings. 21 Do not lose sight of them and keep them within your heart.

Proverbs 4:23 Guard your inner emotions with all watchfullness for from it flows the source and wellspring of all life.

Psalm 139: 14 I praise you for I an fearfully and wonderfully made. Wonderful are you works; my soul knows it well.

Romans 2:11 God does not show partiality toward persons.

Romans 12: 1-2 I beseech you therefore, brethren, by the mercies of God, that you present your bodies a living sacrifice, holy, acceptable to God, which is your reasonable service. 2 And do not be conformed to this world, but be transformed by the renewing of your mind, that you may prove what is that good and acceptable and perfect will of God.

2 Corinthians 5:17 Therefore, if anyone is in Christ, he is a new creation; old things have passed away; behold, all things have become new.

Ephesians 4:2 Always be humble and gentle. Be patient with each other. Make allowance for eah other's faults, because of your love.

Philippians 2:12 Therefore, my beloved, as you have always obeyed, not as in my presence only, but now much more in my absence, work out your own salvation with fear and trembling.

1 Thessalonians 5:11 Therefore, encourage one another and build one another up, just as you are doing.

1 Peter 3:3-4 Your beauty should not come from outward adornment,... 4 But from the inner disposition of your heart, the unfading beauty of a gentle and quiet spirit, which is precious in God's sight.

1 John 3:3 And everyone who has this hope in Him purifies himself, just as He is pure.

Final Thoughts

As we age life seems to present new or unexpected opportunities at every turn. The challenge is to positively exemplify or even codify those events. Unhealthy and distressing situations and seasons filled with trials and tribulations can be overcome and transformed. Remember, nobody on the earth can say they have never considered various choices available or changed in some way, whether consciously or subconsciously. Be sure to look at options and adaptations that mature, raise up, and move mental, emotional, and spiritual growth forward. If you foster those advancing choices and changes, they will bloom and flourish.

Although adopting new options may appear daunting at first, remain consistent. Soldier through to see and feel distinctively brighter differences in mind, body, and soul. Some of you may be drawn to refresh or restore by revisiting sections and sharing with others, as patterns of perseverance become refined. Prior toxic attitudes, influences, and inclinations dissipate, as they are replaced by a peaceful conviction to perspectives, which are more productive.

Some of you may be emboldened to write your own statements of choice to applaud, pursuits of change to accomplish, or recall relevant scriptures of praise to include, as your paradigm shifts. Go for it! Pause, reflect, take time for prayer and meditation, or add your own notes of encouragement and progress. Refer frequently to the humble and sturdy rock of a disciplined ethos deepened in wisdom from God's Word. Overall, I hope and pray this book inspires people to develop a beautiful inner strength and stability mentally, emotionally, in some ways physically, but above all spiritually. Be a witness to ripple effects of change that smooth out and reach the water's edge to effect the greater good.

About the Author

Kathryn Grant celebrates over 20 years as an author, illustrator, presenter and retired teacher for children and adults. Even though she has written and illustrated books for children, as well as a novel of historical fiction about the Civil War, her latest book seeks to bring hope and healing through self-empowering change. *Choices, Changes, Chapter and Verse* is also available in Spanish, as well as her children's book, *The Ants and the Clouds Knew Why.*

Printed in the United States
by Baker & Taylor Publisher Services